Ready to go!

IDEAS FOR DRAMA

KS2

P4 to 7

ACKNOWLEDGEMENTS
The Queen's Printer and Controller of HMSO for material from the National Curriculum, reproduced under the terms of HMSO Guidance Note 8.

Every effort has been made to trace copyright holders and the publishers apologise for any inadvertent omissions.

AUTHOR
Alison Chaplin

DESIGNER
Anna Oliwa

EDITOR
Roanne Davis

ILLUSTRATIONS
Andy Keylock

ASSISTANT EDITOR
Dulcie Booth

COVER ARTWORK
Andy Parker

SERIES DESIGNER
Anna Oliwa

Text © 2001
Alison Chaplin
© 2001 Scholastic Ltd

Designed using Adobe Pagemaker
Published by Scholastic Ltd, Villiers House, Clarendon Avenue, Leamington Spa, Warwickshire CV32 5PR

890   67890

British Library Cataloguing-in-Publication Data
A catalogue record for this book is available from the British Library.

ISBN 0-439-01780-7

Contents

Introduction

Drama is beginning to find an established place in the primary curriculum, within English, and has long been recognized as a subject which benefits the learning and development of young children. There are three main strands to the effective use of drama: a means to build children's confidence and develop their social skills; a teaching approach for exploring cross-curricular subjects and issues; and an aid in developing children's performance and self-presentation skills. These three strands often overlap or interweave, resulting in a learning experience which is productive on many levels simultaneously. Central to all drama work is the concept of 'shared experience', as children learn and work together, and implicit within many lessons is the element of continuous assessment, both of work the children observe and in which they participate. Having the opportunity to learn through drama provides children with skills, knowledge and understanding that cannot be achieved in the same way with any other subject and that feeds into all other areas of their school and personal lives.

ABOUT THIS BOOK

Many of the activities in this book have been designed to provide both teachers and their children with a simple, yet effective, introduction to a variety of drama methods. The activities have been compiled to develop drama approaches from the simplest games to, finally, making provision for drama in accordance with the revised National Curriculum. The framework for drama in the National Curriculum at Key Stage 2 specifies the range of activities and

skills required to ensure effective provision, progression and continuity across the key stages. These are as follows:

RANGE

The range of drama activities should include:
- improvisation and working in role
- scripting and performing plays
- responding to performances.

SKILLS

To participate in a wide range of drama activities and to evaluate their own and others' contributions, children should be taught to:
- create, adapt and sustain different roles, individually and in groups
- use character, action and narrative to convey story, themes, emotions and ideas in plays they devise and script
- use dramatic conventions to explore characters and issues, for example hot-seating, flashback, representing issues in different ways
- evaluate their own and others' contributions to the overall effectiveness of performances.

Many drama activities will focus on more than one of these elements during the same lesson, others will concentrate on developing the social and personal skills of the children, as specified in the additional English curriculum strands of speaking, listening and group discussion and interaction. Sections 4 and 5 of this book provide a stronger focus on the National Curriculum requirements than earlier sections. All of the activities, however, will develop the children's creative, social or personal skills.

Information on how to organize each activity is designed to be easily adapted for the needs of children of different abilities. Ideas for follow-on work should provide enough material for additional lessons and many of the activities require little or no equipment. This all aims to ensure that teachers, regardless of their experience in teaching drama, can use this book with ease and confidence.

IDEAS FOR DRAMA KEY STAGE 1 (P1 TO 3)

The activities in this lead-in book are arranged under the same headings as those in *Ideas for Drama Key Stage 2 (P4 to 7)*, and provide a built-in progression. Some activities are directly linked, either through content or skills, so you are able to select those most appropriate for the abilities and needs of your children.

At both stages, the activities and drama methods specified can be integrated into a variety of curriculum areas.

INTRODUCTORY WARM-UP GAMES

The activities in this section focus on children:
■ getting to know each other
■ developing their concentration, observation and memory skills
■ learning to respond appropriately to instructions
■ interacting positively with others
■ gaining confidence
■ developing their speaking and listening skills.
    The activities are short. They are not intended to be worked through progressively, and can stand alone as simple games or be delivered as warm-ups at the beginning of a longer session, in conjunction with activities from other sections of this book.

WHO'S MISSING?

RESOURCES AND LESSON ORGANIZATION
You will need a medium to large space in which to work. Children work together as a whole class.

WHAT TO DO
Ask the children to each stand in a space. Explain that they are going to play a memory game that will help them to get to know each other. Ask: *Why is this important?* (It helps us to work together well.) Tell the children that you will ask them to move carefully around the area and that on your command of *Drop!* they are to curl into a small ball on the ground and close their eyes. Explain that you will then tap one of them on the back and that this child should then quietly leave the room and hide outside or move to a part of the room where they cannot be seen.

    Now tell the children that on your command of *Move!* the rest of the class should open their eyes, stand and move around the room carefully again. Explain that when you call out the next command, *Freeze*, they should all immediately stand very still and silent and look around to see who is standing in the room with them.

    When the children are all standing still and silent, ask them who is missing and encourage them to give you the name of the absent child. When this has been worked out correctly, repeat the process, completing several turns with different children.

NOW OR LATER
■ Play this in the classroom, with the children at their tables, closing their eyes whilst the selected child leaves the room or hides. Ask the children to change places whilst this child is absent.
■ Insist on the name suggested being correct and accept the first guess only, to encourage the children to think carefully before speaking.
■ Increase the difficulty by asking two or more children to leave the room or hide.
■ 'Reverse' the game: ask two or three children to leave or hide and have two of the remaining children swap places, then ask the first children to return and suggest who has moved.

OBJECTIVES
To enable children to:
■ get to know each other
■ develop observational skills
■ develop memory skills
■ learn each other's names.

CROSS-CURRICULAR LINKS
PSHE
Working co-operatively; developing interpersonal skills; following instructions.

ENGLISH
Responding appropriately to others; developing speaking and listening skills.

NAME CHASE

OBJECTIVES

To enable children to:
■ learn each other's names
■ follow specific instructions
■ gain confidence in group situations.

CROSS-CURRICULAR LINKS

PSHE

Working co-operatively; generating a positive environment; following rules; gaining friendship skills; taking part in discussions.

ENGLISH

Speaking confidently and clearly; responding appropriately to others; developing listening skills.

RESOURCES AND LESSON ORGANIZATION

You will need: a medium to large work space; two beanbags of different colours (or similar soft objects). Children work together as a whole class.

WHAT TO DO

Ask the children to sit in a circle and place one of the beanbags in the centre, giving the other beanbag to one of the children. Explain that they are going to play a game in which they will call out the names of other people in the group. Ask: *Why is it important that we learn each other's names?* (It creates a friendly atmosphere and helps us to work together well.)

Tell the children that the first child holding the beanbag must run into the centre of the circle, swap the beanbags over and then call out the name of another child, handing the second beanbag to them. When the second child has received the beanbag, they should run into the centre of the circle, swap the beanbags over and call out the name of a third child, passing the beanbag to them.

Advise the children that no name can be called out more than once and that the beanbags must be swapped for each turn. Children can call out the name of any child sitting in the circle but the beanbag must be handed to them correctly before they move into the centre of the circle to swap the beanbags over.

Continue playing the game until the name of every child in the circle has been called out and each member of the group has been into the centre, swapped the beanbags and passed one on. The last child to be called should call out the name of the first child who started the game.

Finally, reinforce the children's learning by asking: *Did you enjoy that game? Why? Why not? What did you learn from playing it?* (Each other's names; how to move quickly and how to work well together.)

NOW OR LATER

■ Ask all the children to say each name out loud in advance (or afterwards) to ensure that they know and remember everyone's name.
■ Ask the children to pass the beanbag on to the person sitting next to them, rather than selecting any child.
■ Use additional beanbags and instruct children to call out two names at each turn.
■ Impose a time limit for the game to be completed in and try to beat it each time the game is played.

MATCH UP!

RESOURCES AND LESSON ORGANIZATION

You will need: a small to medium work space; a name card for each child from photocopiable page 10. Children work together as a whole class.

WHAT TO DO

Tell the children that they are going to play a game which relies on them remembering the names of other class members. Ask: *Why is it important to know each other's names?* (We can become friends and work together well.) Write the name of each class member on one of the photocopiable cards. Shuffle and distribute these face down, one to each child, ensuring that no one receives the card with their own name on it. Explain that you will give a countdown from ten and, in that time, they must find the person whose name is on their card and deliver the card to them.

When the children understand what is expected of them, begin the countdown, then, after the count of one, instruct the children to *Stop!* Ask who has received the correct card. Who still has to match their card with its proper owner? If some cards still have to be matched, allow the children a further countdown from five to achieve this. If all cards have been presented correctly, tell the children to turn their cards over again so that the names can no longer be seen and give them these instructions to swap: *Pass your card to the person next to you. Now swap with the person opposite you. Now take two steps to the right and swap cards with the person in front of you. Now take three steps forward and swap with the person on your left.* The cards should now be well shuffled. Repeat the game, giving the children a slow countdown from ten for them to deliver their cards to the rightful owners.

NOW OR LATER

■ Reduce the time limit, allowing children a shorter countdown.
■ Use the blank cards to write different criteria, for example 'someone with brown hair', 'someone with blue eyes' and so on, asking children to find appropriate recipients. Or, ask the children to suggest criteria for additional cards, such as favourite television programmes and favourite foods. Allow extra time if using alternative criteria, so that children can question each other, but gradually reduce the countdown over a number of games.

OBJECTIVES

To enable children to:
■ learn each other's names
■ gain confidence in a group setting
■ consolidate memory skills.

CROSS-CURRICULAR LINKS

PSHE
Working co-operatively; generating a supportive environment; following rules; developing interpersonal skills.

ENGLISH
Responding appropriately to others; communicating effectively; developing speaking and listening skills; reading with purpose.

NAME WHO'S NEXT

OBJECTIVES

To enable children to:
■ get to know each other
■ gain confidence in group situations
■ respond quickly to verbal prompts
■ warm up physically.

CROSS-CURRICULAR LINKS

PSHE

Following rules; working co-operatively; developing interpersonal skills; generating a supportive environment.

ENGLISH

Speaking loudly and clearly; listening to others; responding appropriately to others.

PE

Performing actions with control; meeting challenges; applying rules and conventions.

RESOURCES AND LESSON ORGANIZATION

You will need: a medium to large work space; a beanbag (or similar soft object). Children work together as a whole group.

WHAT TO DO

Ask the children to sit in a circle and hand the beanbag to one of them. Explain that they are going to play a physical game that will help them to get to know each other. Ask: *Why is it important to know each other's names?* (We can become friends and work together well.) Tell the children that when you say *Go!* the person holding the beanbag must leave their place and run in a clockwise direction around the outside of the circle carrying the beanbag. This child should then enter the centre of the circle through their space to place the beanbag on the floor, but before reaching the centre, must call out the name of another child.

The child whose name has been called out must then immediately go to the centre of the circle, pick up the beanbag, leave the circle through their space and run clockwise around the outside, entering back through their space and calling out the name of another child before placing the beanbag back in the centre on the floor.

Make sure the children understand that each child must call out the name of the next participant before placing the beanbag on the floor and no name should be called out twice. It is advisable for children to have two or three names in mind in preparation of their turn, to ensure speedy continuity. Remind the children to take care not to collide when running to and from the centre of the circle, but encourage them to keep a fast pace to the game.

Continue playing until every member of the group has had a turn, with the last child calling out the name of the child who went first.

NOW OR LATER

■ Impose a time limit of, for example, five minutes to complete the game.
■ Try to 'beat the clock' by imposing shorter time limits.
■ Call out the names of two children who then race to reach the beanbag, the winner running around the circle and calling out two more names.
■ Use two beanbags and two names, turning the game into a race to see who returns to the centre first.

INTERVIEWS

RESOURCES AND LESSON ORGANIZATION

You will need: a small to medium work space; interview worksheets from photocopiable pages 11 and 12 for each child; writing materials. Children work individually within the whole class.

WHAT TO DO

Explain to the children that you want them to interview each other, using their interview worksheets. Tell them that they must find people who can give the answer 'yes' to the different questions on their sheets. Explain that, when they receive a positive response, they must write the name of that person next to the question just asked. Advise the children that they cannot, however, write a person's name down more than once and so must find different people in the class to provide 'yes' answers to the questions. Tell the children that they will be given a time limit of five minutes to interview as many people as possible, get as many 'yes' responses as they can, and write down as many different names correctly on their interview sheets.

When the children understand what is expected of them, allow a short time for them to read through the questions, then give them an instruction to begin. Give regular updates on the time remaining, telling the children to stop interviewing when the time limit has elapsed. Count up the number of names written on each sheet and check that the responses are correct. Announce those with the most correct names as the winner or winners and give these children a round of applause.

NOW OR LATER

■ Reduce the time limit allowed for the game.
■ Invite the children to suggest alternative or additional questions for the interview sheets.
■ Ask the children to devise, type and print their own interview sheets. Use these for formal interviews, with the children working in pairs to interview each other.

OBJECTIVES

To enable children to:
■ get to know each other
■ learn each other's names
■ work within time constraints
■ gain confidence in a group setting.

CROSS-CURRICULAR LINKS

PSHE

Developing interpersonal skills; generating a positive environment; respecting differences between people; following rules.

ENGLISH

Responding appropriately to others; asking questions; listening with understanding; speaking confidently; recording information.

ICT

Using equipment for a variety of purposes, including word-processing.

Name cards

Interview questions (1)

1. Do you play football?

Name _____

2. Do you watch *Coronation Street*?

Name _____

3. Have you ever been to America?

Name _____

4. Do you play a musical instrument?

Name _____

5. Do you have a pet?

Name _____

· ·

Question _____

Name _____

Question _____

Name _____

Interview questions (2)

6. Do you enjoy reading?

Name _____

7. Is your birthday in May?

Name _____

8. Do you have a brother?

Name _____

9. Do you like spaghetti?

Name _____

10. Do you have a computer at home?

Name _____

Question _____

Name _____

Question _____

Name _____

MOVEMENT GAMES
AND EXERCISES

The activities in this section focus on children:
- developing spatial awareness
- gaining awareness of how they use their bodies
- interacting physically with each other
- working together in small and large groups
- understanding how to convey situations and roles in mime
- learning how to use movements expressively
- performing in dramatic situations.

These activities introduce children to the various skills required for expressive improvisation and performance. Initial exercises aim to encourage physical contact and develop basic spatial awareness. The section then develops these skills to address specific drama requirements. In that respect, some of the earlier activities could be combined with later ones to form extended lessons.

BODY PARTS

RESOURCES AND LESSON ORGANIZATION

You will need a large space in which to work; photocopiable page 10 (for 'Now or later' activity). Children work together in small groups, then participate in a whole-class discussion.

WHAT TO DO

Ask the children to form groups of six. Explain that they are going to do a physical activity in which only certain parts of their bodies will be allowed to touch the floor. Point out that they will need to work carefully and sensibly with their team members and ask: *Why do you think that's important?* (Otherwise someone will get hurt.) Tell the children that you will call out certain body parts and they must then arrange the people in their group so that only these body parts are making contact with the floor. Ask them: *How can you achieve this?* (By supporting, holding and carrying each other.) Ensure that the children understand that no furniture or external supports are to be used.

Let the children know that the first group who place only the specified body parts on the floor correctly will be named as winners and will gain a point for their team. The team with the most points at the end of the activity will be the overall winners. Encourage the children to work together positively, saying: *You should try to listen to what each group member has to say, because one suggestion might be the solution that wins your team a point.* Tell them that you will give them a limited amount of time to discuss, plan and achieve their positions.

When all of the children understand what is expected of them, work through several combinations of body parts, beginning with those which are fairly simple to achieve and gradually increasing the level of difficulty. Ideas could include:
- four feet and four hands
- three feet and two hands
- four feet, two hands and an elbow
- three feet, one back, two hands and an elbow
- four feet, two knees, two elbows and an ear
- three feet, one hand, two elbows and two bottoms

and so on. You could even specify whether the hands, elbows, knees, and so on should be right or left.

OBJECTIVES
To enable children to:
- reach agreement in group discussions
- plan, explore and evaluate work
- follow specific instructions
- make non-threatening physical contact.

CROSS-CURRICULAR LINKS
PSHE
Working co-operatively in a team situation; taking part in discussions; generating a supportive environment.

ENGLISH
Listening to others; sharing ideas; discussing possibilities and outcomes.

PE
Performing actions with skill; planning and using tactics for small-group activities; problem-solving.

Repeat the activity several times until you have a team who are clear winners. Ask all of the children to sit down in their groups and encourage them to reflect on the activity by asking: *Did you enjoy that? Why? Why not? What do you think you learned from that activity?* (To work with other people, listen to others, co-operate, follow instructions carefully.) *How could this help you when you are doing drama in the future?* (We need to be able to listen carefully to instructions when we are performing; we have to be confident about working with other people when we are performing in plays; we need to be able to share our ideas and know how to plan what we are going to do.)

NOW OR LATER

■ Invite the children to suggest body part combinations.
■ Write different body parts on cards (you could use photocopiable page 10), then ask several children to draw a card each and use these as a basis for the activity.
■ Try the activity with different group sizes, both smaller and larger.

PASS THE SHOE

OBJECTIVES

To enable children to:
■ interact positively with each other
■ understand how their actions affect others
■ make non-threatening physical contact.

RESOURCES AND LESSON ORGANIZATION

You will need: a small to medium work space; a shoe – preferably of soft canvas; chairs (optional). Children work together as a whole class.

WHAT TO DO

Ask the children to sit in a circle. Explain that they are going to pass the shoe to each other in turn, but that you are going to specify *how* they should pass it on. Tell the children that they are *not* allowed to touch the shoe with their hands, and that if it drops to the floor, the shoe must go back two places before it can be passed on again. Hand the shoe to one of the children and tell them that they can pass it in either direction, but that it can only be held and passed using elbows. (Children grip the shoe between their own elbows and their neighbour takes it using their elbows as a 'clamp'.) Encourage the children to pass the shoe slowly and carefully, taking care not to drop it.

When the shoe has made a successful journey around the circle back to the original child, with each child having received it and passed it on, hand it to a different child to start. Instruct the children that this time they are to pass the shoe to each other using only their feet. Again, the rules of not touching or dropping the shoe apply. (This element of the game works better with the children sitting on chairs.) The first child must clamp the shoe firmly between their feet, passing it carefully to the child on their left or right (their choice), who must take it carefully between their feet and pass it on to their neighbour, and so on.

Once this journey has been completed successfully, hand the shoe to another child and ask the children to pass the shoe around using their knees only. This is more difficult, and children need to be advised to take great care when passing and retrieving, to ensure that the shoe doesn't fall. Variations in height make this element of the activity more difficult, so the children need encouragement to think about how they can pass the shoe on effectively to a shorter or taller neighbour.

After this variation has been accomplished, give the shoe to a fourth child and ask the children to pass the shoe using only their shoulders and chins. This is the most difficult modification of all. (The children should clamp the shoe between their chin and shoulder, holding it as firmly as they can whilst still allowing enough of the shoe to remain for the next child to get hold of.) Again, the rules about touching with hands or dropping the shoe apply. Children will probably feel that this task is impossible, and the shoe will drop several times, but they should be encouraged to complete the task.

When the shoe has finally made it successfully around the circle, tell that children that you now want them to pass it around again, but that this time they can pass it in any way they wish, as long as this is not in the same manner as it was passed to them. If the shoe was passed to them using elbows, they cannot retrieve it or pass it on using their elbows – it must be collected and passed on using a different part of the body. Tell the children that they can use any of the methods they have already used, or use an alternative of their own choosing. Remind them though that the rules about not touching the shoe with their hands and it going back two places if it drops still apply. Hand the shoe to a fifth and final child, asking them to begin by passing it to the child on their left or right (their choice).

Encourage the children to work co-operatively to ensure that the shoe continues its journey around the circle without being touched or dropped, and praising those children who try to assist their neighbours receiving the shoe. When the shoe has returned to the original child, praise the children for their efforts and invite them to applaud themselves if the shoe made a successful journey around the circle.

Finally, lead a brief discussion, asking the children to suggest what they might have learned from this activity and how these skills might be applied to other areas of their school life.

NOW OR LATER

Use music to accompany the shoe's journey, with children changing the method of passing the shoe each time the music stops.

SPOT THE LEADER

RESOURCES AND LESSON ORGANIZATION

You will need a medium to large space in which to work. Children work together as a whole class.

WHAT TO DO

Ask the children to stand in a circle, and explain that one of them will lead the rest of the group in a series of movements. Tell the children that another child, who has been asked to leave the room or hide, will then guess who is leading the movements. Explain that the person who hides will not know who the leader of the movements is and the rest of the children are to copy the movements of the leader without giving away who this person is.

The leader should perform simple, repetitive movements for the others to copy, for example clapping hands, stamping feet, crossing and uncrossing arms. It is advisable to discourage leaders from performing jumping moves, as this creates a lot of noise and very quickly becomes exhausting! Movements performed by the leader should change every 20 seconds or so. Ask the children: *How can you copy the different movements without giving away who the leader is?* (You can try to avoid direct eye contact, or follow other people in the group as they change to a new movement.)

When all of the children understand the activity rules, select one child to either leave the room or go where they cannot see the rest of the group. Now silently select another child to lead the movements. Ask this child to raise their hand so that everyone is sure about who they are following and advise the leader to be very careful how and when they change their movements, so that the person guessing doesn't see them doing it. Instruct the leader to begin their first movement, calling

the absent child back in as soon as this begins. Ask the child who is guessing to stand in the centre of the circle and allow them up to three attempts at guessing who the leader is. Repeat the activity several times, selecting a new guesser and leader each time.

Finally, encourage the children to reflect on the activity by asking: *Did you enjoy that? Why? Why not? What do you think you learned from that activity?* (We learned to work together; to trust each other, to perform actions carefully and to think about how we moved.)

NOW OR LATER

■ Nominate two children to guess.
■ Ask the children to stand apart from each other, instead of in a circle, to make the activity more difficult.
■ Ask the leader to perform simple mimes, for example getting dressed, washing a window and so on.
■ Specify the movements or mimes to be used and link these to actions from a particular text or story read by the children, for example Cinderella cleaning in the kitchen, the wolf blowing down the little pigs' house.

SILLY WALKS

RESOURCES AND LESSON ORGANIZATION

You will need: a large work space; suitable music (see 'What to do' – Sousa's *Liberty Bells* is ideal) and equipment to play it. Children work together as a whole class.

WHAT TO DO

Play the music to the children, asking them to listen carefully and assess it with regard to its mood (happy/sad), tempo (fast/slow) and dynamics (loud/quiet). Now ask the children to find a space and say: *I want you to move around the room to the music and change your movements each time there are changes in the music.* Suggest that, for example, they could begin by marching then change to walking, then to running, hopping, skipping, and so on.

When the children have performed their movements for a short time, stop them and explain that you will now play the music again and that this time you want them

OBJECTIVES

To enable children to:
■ gain confidence in a group situation
■ use movement expressively
■ create different roles
■ use movements to express characters.

17

to move around the room using silly or exaggerated movements. Encourage them to make their walks as ridiculous and unusual as possible: throwing their legs and arms out, bending low then stepping high and so on. Remind them that they should again move in time with the music and say: *Don't worry about looking silly, just concentrate on your own movements and making sure that you don't bump into anyone else.* Tell them that each time the tempo, mood or volume of the music changes, they must change their silly walk for a different type of silly walk.

Finally, encourage the children's reflections by asking: *Did you enjoy that? Why? Why not? What do you think you learned from the activity?* (Not to be embarrassed; to listen carefully to music; to move in different ways; to use our imaginations.)

NOW OR LATER
■ Allow some of the children to show their silly walks to the others.
■ Invite suggestions of other types of movement which could express the music.
■ Ask the children to suggest character types indicated by the music and devise movements for these.
■ Encourage the children to explore alternative ways of moving to the music, for example not using their feet, moving backwards, moving high and low.
■ Select alternative pieces of music for the activity.

CIRCLE SILLY WALKS

OBJECTIVES
To enable children to:
■ gain confidence in a group situation
■ interact positively with each other
■ follow specific instructions
■ use movement expressively.

RESOURCES AND LESSON ORGANIZATION
You will need a medium to large space in which to work. Children work together as a whole class.

WHAT TO DO
Ask the children to stand in a circle. Explain that you will ask one of them to use a funny or silly walk to travel across the circle to another child, whom they must touch. The touched child must then also travel across the circle to touch another child, first copying the first silly walk and then changing it. The third child, again, copies the new silly walk, then changes it and passes that on to a fourth person. This process should continue until everyone in the circle has passed a silly walk on, with the last child touching the child who crossed first.

18

Tell the children that the changes made to silly walks can be as subtle or exaggerated as they wish, but make sure they remember to have some consideration for the person they are passing the silly walk on to and take care not to make the movements too difficult. If children struggle to make changes to their walks in the short time it takes to cross the circle, instruct them to walk around the inside of the circle first, before passing their walk on.

When they have completed the activity, encourage the children to reflect on it by asking: *Did you enjoy doing that? Why? Why not? What have you learned?* (To not be shy in front of others; to be considerate to other people; to use our bodies in an interesting way; to think and use our imaginations quickly.)

NOW OR LATER

■ Use suitable accompanying music to inspire – many marches by Sousa will be ideal.
■ Ask the children to perform the activity standing in lines opposite to each other, with alternate children taking turns to walk across.
■ Choose two children to start, so that two walks are being passed on at the same time, requiring more concentration.
■ Use character movements as a starting point, and see how exaggerated they become by the end of the activity!

MOVEMENT RELAY

RESOURCES AND LESSON ORGANIZATION
You will need a large space in which to work. Children work in small teams.

WHAT TO DO
Ask the children to form teams of four to six and to line up behind their team members, facing the opposite end of the room. Explain that they are going to have a team relay race where each member of the team uses a different method of movement to travel from their starting position to the other end of the room and back. Give them some suggestions of different movement styles, for example running, running backwards, walking, hopping, skipping, jumping and crawling. Point out that it is acceptable for members from *different* teams to move in the same way.

Explain that the next team member in line cannot go until the person in front of them returns and releases them, by either touching their hand or crossing a specified

CROSS-CURRICULAR LINKS
PSHE
Working co-operatively; developing interpersonal skills; generating a supportive atmosphere.

ENGLISH
Listening to others; sharing experiences; responding appropriately to others.

OBJECTIVES
To enable children to:
■ work in and out of role
■ follow specific instructions
■ use movement expressively.

CROSS-CURRICULAR LINKS
PSHE
Developing interpersonal skills; following rules; working co-operatively; facing challenges in a positive, supportive environment.

ENGLISH
Listening to others; discussing and planning outcomes; sharing ideas; taking turns in speaking.

PE
Planning and adopting small-team tactics; problem-solving; working with others to meet challenges; performing actions with control.

point or line. Tell the children to plan their individual team movements carefully, saying: *You might want to take a few seconds to discuss how each member of your team plans to move so that you don't waste time trying to sort out a different method of movement during the race.* Allow them up to two minutes for these planning discussions to take place.

When the children are all ready, start the relay race, watching carefully throughout for children who are not adhering to the rules properly. At the end, congratulate the winning team and, if time permits, allow the children to race again. This enables them to refine their tactics and plan their strategies for winning with more precision.

Afterwards, gather the children together and encourage them to reflect on the activity by asking: *Did you enjoy that? Why? Why not? What do you think you learned from taking part in that activity?* (To work together, to plan and share ideas, to follow rules) Then ask: *What did (or would) you do differently the next time you raced?* (Take more time to plan properly and make sure to use quick movements at the beginning and the end of the race.)

NOW OR LATER
■ Be specific about the movement styles allowed, for example no feet, only moving backwards, no running and so on.
■ Use character types as the basis for the movements, for example an elderly person, a teenager, a police officer, a baby.
■ Select teams yourself, putting children with those they are less familiar with rather than friends to encourage them to interact with others.

FREEZE IT!

OBJECTIVES
To enable children to:
■ follow and respond to specific instructions
■ appreciate the concept of physical control
■ generate a positive atmosphere
■ gain confidence in a group situation
■ use movement effectively
■ use actions to express emotions.

RESOURCES AND LESSON ORGANIZATION
You will need a large work space. A whistle might be useful. Children work together as a whole class.

WHAT TO DO
Ask the children to walk around the room carefully, without touching or bumping into anyone else, and explain that, when you shout *Freeze!* (or blow your whistle), they are to stand as still and as silent as possible. Any children moving or making a noise after your command is given should be asked to sit down and take no further part in that stage of the activity.

When you have repeated this process several times, ask all of the children to stand in a space (including those children who were 'out') and then tell them that they are now going to repeat the activity, but this time they are to walk backwards around the room. Advise them to move cautiously and take care not to touch or bump into anyone. Again, when you blow your whistle, or give the *Freeze!* command, they are to stand still and silent.

Now repeat the activity another two or three times, instructing children to move around the room in different ways each time, for example hopping, crawling, skipping or jumping. In each turn, children who do not stand completely still and silent when your command is given should be asked to sit down.

Finally, encourage the children to reflect on the activity by asking: *Did you enjoy that? Why? Why not? Was it difficult to do? What did you find difficult about it? What do you think you learned from it?* (To control our movements, to follow instructions immediately, to take care when working with others, to respond to the *freeze* command.) Encourage them to consider their drama skills by asking: *How can this activity help you when you are doing drama?* (It helps to control movements, to concentrate, to be aware of people around us; it develops the ability to hold positions needed for creating tableaux.)

NOW OR LATER

■ Play appropriate music for the children to move to, instructing them to freeze when the music stops.
■ Rather than playing as an elimination game, use the activity as a basis for encouraging children to develop their 'freezing' skills by praising those children who freeze well.
■ Ask the children to show a particular emotion when they freeze, such as horror, excitement, sadness, joy, pain, or fear.

TIME TRAVEL

RESOURCES AND LESSON ORGANIZATION

You will need a large space in which to work. Children respond individually within a whole-class setting.

WHAT TO DO

Ask the children to sit in a space. Explain that they are going to go on an imaginary journey back through time in a time machine and say: *I want you to imagine that you are sitting in your time machine. Make yourself comfortable in your seat and decide what period in time you want to travel to – it could be any time in history.* Allow time here to lead a brief discussion with the children about which periods of history would be interesting to visit (these could be linked to areas being covered in your schemes of work). Explain that they will be invisible to any people they meet on their time travels.

When you feel the children are all confident about what time period they will visit, continue the narrative by saying: *Have a look around your time machine, checking all of your controls and instrument panels. In a moment you will start your machine and you will be transported to your chosen time in history.* Allow time for the children to respond to this narrative by looking around their time machine and then ask: *Are you all ready to time travel? Right, 3, 2, 1, off you go!* Encourage the children to mime their reactions to their fictional settings and allow a short amount of time for this.

Then say: *You have now landed in your chosen time in history. Climb slowly out of your time machine and take a look around outside. What can you see?* Invite the children to describe what they see when they step out of their time machines by asking, for example: *Do you see any buildings? What are they like? Are there any people around? What are they doing?* Take responses from as many children as possible, acknowledging and commenting on their descriptions as appropriate. Encourage

CROSS-CURRICULAR LINKS
PSHE
Following rules; facing challenges; identifying their achievements; taking part in discussions.

ENGLISH
Listening to others; speaking confidently in group situations; sharing ideas and experiences.

PE
Performing actions with control.

OBJECTIVES
To enable children to:
■ respond as themselves in a fictional setting
■ use actions to convey situations
■ sequence and develop scenes
■ reflect on their performances
■ gain confidence in a supportive atmosphere.

CROSS-CURRICULAR LINKS
PSHE
Generating a positive atmosphere; facing challenges; developing cognitive skills.

ENGLISH
Listening to others; sustaining concentration; sharing ideas; creating and describing imaginative experiences.

HISTORY
Using dates and historical vocabulary; communicating knowledge and understanding of history.

them to take time to observe their new environments carefully, prompting them to respond with both actions and verbal answers to any questions asked.

Allow sufficient time for the children to explore and describe the period they are visiting and then say: *It is now time for you to return to the present again. Return to your time machine.* Pause to enable them to mime this as they may have travelled some distance from their machines. *Climb back inside and prepare yourself for returning, setting today's date on your instrument panel.* Allow more time for the children to mime these actions and then say: *Are you all ready to return to the present? Right, 3, 2, 1, return!* Finish with the children returning to the present and stepping out of their time machines.

Now, encourage the children to reflect on the lesson by asking: *Did you enjoy that? What did you enjoy about it? Was it difficult to imagine what the historical time you visited looked like?* Ask for volunteers to describe what they saw on their time travels. Allow as much time as possible for the children to describe their historical visits, encouraging them to describe sounds and smells as well. Then go on to ask: *Do you think that you were acting today?* (Yes.) *Why was that acting?* (We were using our imaginations to pretend to be somewhere else.) *Do we pretend like this in any other situations?* (Yes, when we make up stories or act in plays and have to pretend that the situation is real.)

NOW OR LATER
■ Encourage the children to describe their journey in greater detail.
■ Ask the children to draw or write a description of their time travel journey and the scene when they arrived.
■ Take the children as a whole class on a journey to visit a specified period in history.
■ Make a similar time travel journey into the future.

THE MAGIC TOY-BOX

OBJECTIVES
To enable children to:
■ create and sustain roles individually and in groups
■ improvise and work in role
■ develop scenes and incidents
■ use actions to convey character
■ reflect on drama in which they have participated.

RESOURCES AND LESSON ORGANIZATION
You will need: a large work space; the story on photocopiable page 25. Children respond individually within a whole-class setting.

WHAT TO DO
Ask the children to stand in a space, and explain that they are going to mime the actions of different types of characters from a story extract you are going to read to them. Tell them that you want them to listen carefully for all the different characters in the story and what they do, and to mime their different movements and actions.

22

Explain that they will all act as all of the different characters at the same time. They will need to listen carefully to your narrative and work in their own spaces to react to what they hear with appropriate mimes.

When all of the children understand what is expected of them, begin reading the narrative 'The magic toy-box'. Read slowly and pause occasionally to give the children time to react.

When the story is finished, use the remaining time to evaluate the activity by asking the children: *Which character did you enjoy being? Why? Did you find it easy to pretend to be these different characters? Which was the most difficult to do? Why? Was that acting?* (Yes, because we were pretending to be someone and somewhere else.) *How could we make our acting more believable?* (By using our faces and bodies more expressively to show where we are, who we are, what we are doing and how we feel about the situation.)

CROSS-CURRICULAR LINKS
PSHE
Developing interpersonal skills; facing and meeting challenges; developing cognitive skills; speaking in front of an audience.

ENGLISH
Listening to others; responding appropriately to others; speaking confidently and clearly; sharing ideas and experiences.

Section 2

NOW OR LATER
■ Invite some children to show others their mimes for the different characters.
■ If you have time, use the final evaluation to repeat the activity, encouraging the children to be more effective in their use of facial expressions, actions and body language.
■ Ask the children to consider 'what happened next'. Organize them into small groups to improvise (act out with actions and dialogue) the next part of the story.
■ Ask the children to select one of the characters and prepare an improvisation based on that character.
■ Encourage the children to continue the story in writing.
■ Help the children to write their improvisations as playscripts.

MIME THE STORY

RESOURCES AND LESSON ORGANIZATION
You will need: a large work space; a copy for each child of Aesop's fable 'The travellers and the bear' on photocopiable page 26. Children work in small groups then take part in a whole-class discussion.

WHAT TO DO
Organize the children into groups of four (or three where necessary). Read the story through, with the children following on their copies, and then explain that you are going to ask them to act out the story in mime. Tell the children that the story must

OBJECTIVES
To enable children to:
■ work in role
■ present drama to an audience
■ use character and action to convey a story
■ use drama to explore texts
■ respond to performances.

23

CROSS-CURRICULAR
LINKS
PSHE
Working co-operatively in a
group; developing
interpersonal skills; taking
part in discussions; facing
challenges in a supportive
environment.

ENGLISH
Listening and responding
appropriately to others;
reading aloud; speaking
confidently and clearly;
evaluating and responding to
drama.

be narrated (read aloud) whilst it is being performed, but that the actors cannot use dialogue, only actions, to convey what happens.

Explain to the children that they must work together in their groups to decide what roles are appointed to whom and that this distribution must be achieved fairly, and quickly, as you will impose a time limit of ten minutes for them to plan and rehearse their performances.

Tell the children that, at the end of the rehearsal time, each group will show the rest of the class their story mimes. When all of the children understand what is expected of them, ask the groups to begin organizing their performances, and move around the room ensuring that all of the children are working together and resolving arguments where necessary. (The narrator in any groups of three will have to both narrate and act.) Give regular updates on the amount of time remaining for rehearsal and be strict about adhering to the time limit.

When this has elapsed, designate one area of the room as the performance area and ask each group in turn to perform their story mimes. Encourage the audience to show respect and consideration by remaining silent whilst others are performing and lead them in applauding each group's efforts.

When all of the groups have performed, encourage the children to reflect on the session by asking: *Did you enjoy that? What did you enjoy about it? What did you find difficult?* (Answers may include negotiating roles!) *Were the mimes effective and realistic? Could we have understood what was happening if the story wasn't being read out? How can we make our performances more effective and realistic?* (By using more facial expression, stronger and clearer body language and making character interaction more distinctive.)

NOW OR LATER

■ Encourage the children to turn their mimes into improvisations with both actions and dialogue.

■ Invite suggestions on what the moral of the story might be. (Adversity tests the sincerity of friends.)

■ Ask the children to devise and perform improvisations with the same moral, but set in a modern context.

■ Ask the children to mime other stories, with the audience guessing both content and message.

■ Explore other fables by Aesop in the same manner.

The magic toy-box

Mr Green was very tired. He rubbed his eyes wearily, yawned and then prepared to leave the shop. Taking one last look around to make sure that everything was in order, he put on his big, heavy, black coat, wrapped his scarf around his neck and turned off the shop lights. He stepped out of the door, locking it carefully behind him, and trudged slowly home.

The shop was left in darkness. The big teddy sat on the shelf, his hands resting in his fluffy brown lap; the baby doll lay in the pram, all covered up with woolly blankets, and in the middle of the room, lit by a street lamp, was the huge wooden toy-box. Suddenly, the lid of the toy-box began to open slowly, creaking ever so slightly, and out jumped a toy soldier and then another. They marched to the end of the toy-box and opened the lid fully, calling into the box, "It's all right, he's gone. You can come out now!" And signalling to the other toys inside.

Four more toy soldiers marched quickly out of the toy-box, their heads held high and their backs ramrod straight. Following them came two Beanie Babies, all floppy and wobbly and moving on their hands and knees. Next came a tank and an armoured car driven by two action toys with serious faces; they looked around cautiously and carefully, checking for the enemy.

Gradually, more and more toys came out of the magic toy-box: ballerina dolls, pirouetting gracefully; clown dolls, tripping, tumbling and falling as they climbed out; big, soft cuddly toys carrying piles of building bricks and moving slowly on their chubby little legs; racing cars zooming about like mad things, dashing from one side of the room to the other.

One by one, all of the toys came out of the toy-box and gathered in a group on the shop floor. The teddy climbed down from his place on the shelf, hanging carefully by his paws until he built up enough courage to let himself go and drop to the floor, and the baby doll pushed off her covers and climbed out of her pram, moving slowly and carefully down its side and onto the wheel before making a little jump to the ground.

Eventually, all the toys were assembled together and the first toy soldier, standing up straight, clapped his hands for silence. "Welcome, everyone," he said. "Let's talk about our plans for tonight."

The travellers and the bear

Two friends were travelling on the same road together when they met with a bear. One traveller, in great fear and without a thought for his companion, climbed up into a tree and hid himself. The other, seeing that he had no chance, single-handed, against the bear, had no option but to throw himself on the ground and pretend to be dead; for he had heard that a bear will never touch a dead body. As he lay thus, the bear came up to his head, muffling and snuffling at his nose and ears and heart, but the man immovably held his breath and the beast, supposing him to be dead, shuffled away.

When the bear was almost out of sight, the traveller's companion came down from the tree and asked what it was that the bear had whispered to him. "For," he said, "I observed he put his mouth very close to your ear."

"Why," replied the other, "it was no great secret. He only bade me have a care how I keep company with those who, when they get into difficulty, leave their friends in the lurch."

Section 3 — LANGUAGE AND VOCAL SKILLS

The activities in this section focus on children:
■ speaking aloud in a group context
■ listening to others speak
■ providing appropriate verbal responses
■ responding to instructions
■ using language expressively
■ conveying situations, characters and emotions through language and sound.

   The basic exercises at the beginning of this section encourage children to speak aloud in a group and prepare them for using language and sound expressively. Some of the activities focus on a whole-class choral approach, whilst others develop individual language skills. Activities from the beginning of the section can be combined with later ones to create longer, more intensive sessions.

TALK IT THROUGH

RESOURCES AND LESSON ORGANIZATION
You will need a medium to large space in which to work. Children work in pairs, then small groups, and then take part in a whole-class discussion.

WHAT TO DO
Ask the children to find a partner, sit in a space and label themselves 'A' or 'B'. Explain that they are going to do an activity that involves both partners talking at the same time. 'A's will describe in detail everything they did from waking up this morning until now and 'B's will describe in detail a holiday or outing that they have had (when it was is not important).

   Tell the children that they are both to talk at the same time, and should try to concentrate on their own stories *and* the accounts being related to them by their partners. They should begin talking on your command *Go!* and continue until you give the command *Stop!*

   When all of the children understand what you want them to do, give the *Go!* command and allow the children to continue talking for up to two minutes before saying, *Stop!* Ask the children: *Who managed to continue talking all the time until I said 'Stop'? How many of you managed to hear anything that was said by your partner? What did your partners say?*

   Now ask the children to form groups of four, with two 'A's and two 'B's. Repeat the process, but this time with 'A's describing their holiday or outing and 'B's describing their day from waking up this morning. Give the same *Go!* and *Stop!* commands, allowing the conversations to run for up to two minutes again before repeating the questions to see who could keep talking and how much of the accounts was heard and understood.

   Finally, ask the children to reflect on what they have been working on by asking: *Did you enjoy that? Why? Did you find anything difficult about doing it? What do you think that activity teaches us?* (It helps in concentrating on what we're saying and in not being distracted; it helps in trying to concentrate on what other people are saying; it teaches us how to speak aloud and listen carefully; we learn to work spontaneously.) *How can these skills help when we're performing?* (We need to be able to concentrate on speaking our lines in plays and listening to other people saying their lines without being distracted.)

OBJECTIVES
To enable children to:
■ develop concentration skills
■ use language effectively
■ develop spontaneity and improvisation skills
■ respond to instructions
■ work positively with others.

CROSS-CURRICULAR LINKS
PSHE
Working co-operatively; following rules; meeting challenges; taking part in discussions; developing interpersonal skills.

ENGLISH
Listening to others; speaking audibly and confidently; communicating effectively.

NOW OR LATER
■ Invite the children to suggest other subjects which they could talk about and repeat the activity using these.
■ Ask the children to form groups of three, with 'A' and 'B' trying to prevent 'C' from talking (without using force).
■ Use the same process with children reading a story aloud and others trying to distract them.

TELL THE STORY

OBJECTIVES
To enable children to:
■ use language effectively
■ react spontaneously
■ develop self-confidence
■ use their imaginations.

CROSS-CURRICULAR LINKS
PSHE
Developing interpersonal skills; working co-operatively; generating a supportive environment following instructions; speaking confidently in front of others.

ENGLISH
Developing speaking and listening skills; storytelling; using descriptive language; increasing vocabulary.

RESOURCES AND LESSON ORGANIZATION
You will need: a small to medium work space; a beanbag, small stick or similar object. Children work together as a whole class.

WHAT TO DO
Sit in a circle with the children and explain that they are going to relate the story of Cinderella (or another story which is familiar to them). Tell the children that they will take turns in telling the story and that they can only speak when holding the beanbag (or stick). They must tell at least one sentence of the story whilst holding the object and then pass it on to someone else in the group, who will continue telling the story before passing the object on to another child.

Advise the children that they should speak loudly and clearly and must listen carefully at all times to what others before them have related, so that they do not duplicate parts of the story. Similarly, they can add details that have been omitted by others if they notice these omissions.

Make sure the children understand that the object cannot be passed on until at least one sentence has been added to the story by the person holding it and it can then be given to any person in the group, but not to the same person twice. Encourage the children to be fair and considerate to others by telling as much of the story as they can before passing the object on, and ensuring that details are as full and sequential as possible.

When the children understand what is expected of them, hand the object to a confident child to start telling the story of Cinderella. Allow the object to be passed around the group, supporting and assisting children where necessary. If all of the children have held the object before the story is completed, return the object to the first child and continue until the story is finished.

When the story has been told, encourage the children to reflect on the activity by asking: *Did you enjoy that? Why? Why not? What do you think that activity teaches you?* (To concentrate, listen carefully and use our imaginations; to be fair and considerate to other people.)

Now or later

■ With less confident children, pass the object around yourself, handing it on when you sense they are struggling.
■ Use the same process with other familiar stories.
■ Pass the object around the circle from child to child in a clockwise direction, avoiding children having to decide whom to pass it on to.
■ Use the same process with the children making up their own story.
■ Reduce the number of words spoken by each child, until they are creating 'one-word-each' stories.

CATEGORIES

RESOURCES AND LESSON ORGANIZATION
You will need a small to medium space in which to work. Children work together as a whole class.

WHAT TO DO
Ask the children to stand in a circle, and explain that they are going to play a game in which they name as many items as they can in certain categories that you will give them. Tell the children that they must give an answer in turn, one person at a time, and that if they hesitate a long time before giving an answer, or repeat an answer already given, they will be 'out' and should sit down. Encourage the children to speak loudly and clearly, so that others can hear the answer they have given and avoid repetition.

Begin by asking the children to name different colours, selecting a child to start and then working around the circle in a clockwise direction, with each child naming a different colour. Continue until the majority of the children are 'out' and you have a winner or winners.

Repeat the process using other categories, for example animals; things found at the seaside; vegetables; flowers; modes of transport; television comedy programmes.

Finally, encourage the children to reflect on the activity by asking: *Did you find that difficult? Why? Why not? What do you think that activity teaches you?* (To listen and speak carefully; to think quickly; to remember what other people have said; to think carefully about what we are saying.)

OBJECTIVES
To enable children to:
■ respond spontaneously
■ develop concentration and memory skills
■ use language effectively
■ follow specific instructions
■ gain confidence in a group setting.

CROSS-CURRICULAR LINKS
PSHE

Facing and meeting challenges; following rules; working co-operatively; generating a supportive environment; speaking aloud.

ENGLISH

Developing speaking and listening skills; taking turns in speaking; increasing vocabulary.

NOW OR LATER

■ Invite the children to suggest other categories.
■ Link the categories with other topics being covered.
■ Turn the activity into a team game, with teams writing down as many items in a category as they can within a given time, and the winning team being the one with the most answers.

INSTRUCTIONS

OBJECTIVES

To enable children to:
■ use language effectively
■ use actions and mime to convey situations
■ present drama
■ develop concentration.

CROSS-CURRICULAR LINKS

PSHE

Gaining self-confidence; setting and achieving challenges; generating a supportive environment.

ENGLISH

Listening to others; developing speaking skills; using descriptive language; extending vocabulary.

RESOURCES AND LESSON ORGANIZATION

You will need: a small to medium work space; instruction cards from photocopiable page 34. Children work in pairs within a whole-class setting.

WHAT TO DO

Select two volunteers, asking one child to stand in a space and handing the other child one of the instruction cards. Tell the child with the card that you want them to instruct their partner to perform the task noted, without using the words specified on the card. Advise them that they can use any other words to help them to explain what they want their partner to do.

The second child must silently respond to any instructions given by the first child and mime the actions accordingly. Tell them that they must not work independently, but follow the instructions given by the first child, pausing and waiting for assistance if difficulties arise.

Encourage the children observing to remain quiet whilst the activity is taking place, to support those children involved. When the mime has been performed successfully, give the children a round of applause, select two more volunteers and repeat the process.

Afterwards, encourage reflection on the activity by asking the children: *Did you enjoy that? Why? Why not? What did you find difficult about it? What do you think the activity is teaching you?* (To speak clearly; to consider how we use language; to respond carefully to instructions; to be quiet as an audience and consider others.)

NOW OR LATER

■ Invite the children to suggest other tasks and 'forbidden' words to go with them.
■ Ask all the children to work in pairs simultaneously, and then invite some to show their work to the rest of the class.
■ Increase the number of prohibited words to make the task more difficult.

JUST A MINUTE

OBJECTIVES

To enable children to:
■ think and react spontaneously
■ develop memory and verbal skills
■ follow specific instructions
■ use language effectively.

RESOURCES AND LESSON ORGANIZATION

You will need: a small to medium work space; cards from photocopiable pages 35–7; a stopwatch. Children work individually within a whole-class context.

WHAT TO DO

Ask the children to sit in a semicircle. Select one child to stand or sit at the front of the class. Give this child one of the cards with the name and picture of an object, activity, living thing or type of food on it. Instruct this child to talk to the others for one minute about what is on the card, but insist that they cannot repeat any words, hesitate for too long whilst talking or move away from the subject they are talking about. They can, however, repeat the name of their subject (what is on their card) as many times as they wish. Tell the children sitting in the semicircle to listen carefully for

CROSS-CURRICULAR LINKS
PSHE
Following rules; setting simple goals; learning from experiences; listening to other people.

ENGLISH
Using descriptive language; listening to adults giving explanations; speaking to different people.

any of these rules being broken and to either put their hand up or call out when the speaker does not adhere to the rules.

Allow the child preparing to speak up to 30 seconds to think about what they are going to say and how they are going to say it. Then count them in and ask them to begin speaking about the subject on their card, timing their effort carefully. As soon as the speaker has been noticed making a mistake that breaks a rule, thank them, praise their efforts and note their time. Ask for another volunteer to repeat the process, using the same card again or a different one. Time each speaker and announce the winning child (the one who has spoken for the longest time without breaking any of the rules) at the end of the activity. Thank all of the children for their efforts and lead a brief discussion about the skills the children have learned through taking part in the activity, and how these skills can be applied to other areas of their school life.

Now or later

■ For younger or less confident children, remove the rules and instruct them to just speak on the subject for one minute without hesitating. This will be a difficult achievement in itself.
■ Link the subjects on the cards to other programmes of study, topics or stories.
■ Extend the time limit, either with or without the rules.
■ Ask the children to suggest different subjects for others to talk about.
■ Invite the children to think of some alternative rules, for example not mentioning what is on the card by name, talking with their eyes closed, not saying certain words, such as 'and'.

Telephone calls

Resources and lesson organization
You will need a medium to large work space. Children work in pairs, followed by small groups, then take part in a whole-class discussion.

What to do
Ask the children to find a partner and a space to work in. Explain that you are going to ask them to hold imaginary telephone conversations with each other. Instruct the children to label themselves 'A' and 'B'. 'A's will begin the telephone call, to speak to 'B's about anything they like. This could be, for example: to ask if they'd like to go out

OBJECTIVES

To enable children to:
■ work in role
■ improvise situations
■ develop and sustain characters
■ use language expressively
■ present drama
■ evaluate effectiveness of performances.

Section 3

CROSS-CURRICULAR LINKS

PSHE
Working co-operatively; gaining self-confidence; generating a supportive atmosphere; speaking in front of an audience.

ENGLISH
Developing speaking and listening skills; responding appropriately to others; taking turns in speaking.

somewhere; to ask for help with homework; to invite them to a party; to complain about their behaviour, or any other reason the children can think of why they might call someone on the telephone.

Allow the children up to 30 seconds to consider what their improvised telephone calls will be about and then ask them to begin acting out their conversations. Move from pair to pair, encouraging and advising as appropriate.

After two minutes of these conversations, ask the children to stop and instruct 'B's to begin a different telephone call with their partners. Again, allow these to continue for up to two minutes and then ask the children to stop talking.

Now tell the children that you want 'A's to imagine that they are a customer who has ordered something from a shop, a catalogue or on the Internet which hasn't arrived. 'B's are to be members of the customer services department dealing with the angry customers. Allow the children up to 30 seconds to plan and prepare their improvisations and then ask them to begin, letting the conversations continue for up to two minutes. Then ask the children to swap roles, so that 'A's are now from customer services and 'B's are angry customers. Ask the children to chose a different situation for their conversations and then allow them to continue for up to two minutes again.

Now ask each pair to join with another to make a group of four and to label themselves 'A', 'B', 'C' and 'D'. Explain that you want them to imagine that 'D's are hosts of a radio phone-in show and 'A's, 'B's and 'C's are people calling the radio station with their opinions. Give the children up to two minutes to decide what subject their phone-in is about and what the opinions are of the different people making the telephone calls. Then instruct them to perform their improvisations (the whole class should perform at the same time).

Finally, encourage the children to reflect on the activity by asking: *Did you enjoy doing that? Why? Why not? What did you enjoy most? What was difficult? Do you think your conversations were realistic? Why? Why not? What could you do to make your performances more realistic?* (Act more in character; use our voices more expressively; think more carefully about what we are saying and how we are saying it; plan our improvisations more carefully.)

NOW OR LATER

■ Invite some of the groups to show their radio phone-in improvisations to the others.
■ Specify other subjects for telephone calls or phone-in discussions.
■ Ask the children to devise and perform a short improvisation based upon someone making a telephone call.

SOUNDSCAPES

RESOURCES AND LESSON ORGANIZATION
You will need: a large work space; situation cards from photocopiable page 38. Children work in small groups then participate in a whole-class discussion.

WHAT TO DO
Ask the children to form groups of between four and six and to find a space to work in. Give each group one of the situation cards and ask them to create a 'freeze' (tableau) that represents the scene or situation written on that card. Tell the children that they can interpret the title in any way they wish, but must remember that the picture will be completely still and silent, so simplicity may be more suitable than complex ideas.

Allow the groups up to three minutes to discuss, plan and devise their frozen pictures. Then ask each group to present their tableau in turn to the rest of the class. Encourage the children observing to guess what the title of each picture is.

When the title of each freeze has been guessed ask the groups to recreate them, but this time adding suitable sound effects. The children should perform these accompanying sounds whilst holding their frozen positions. Invite the children to take some time to discuss what sounds might be heard in their particular scene and to ensure that everyone in their group contributes to creating the soundscapes. Give them up to three minutes to create the accompanying soundscapes for their tableau, and then view each one in turn again.

Finally, encourage the children to reflect on and evaluate the session by asking: *Did you enjoy that activity? Why? Why not? Were the tableaux realistic? What made them so? Do you think the sound effects were suitable for the pictures? Why? Why not? What other sounds could have been included, if any? What have you learned from taking part in this activity?* (To work well with each other; to use our bodies expressively; to use our voices effectively; to act without using movement or dialogue.)

NOW OR LATER
■ Invite the children to suggest other titles to create freezes of and repeat the activity using these suggestions.
■ Split the class into two large groups, give each one a tableau to create and ask half of each group to create the frozen picture whilst the rest provide sound effects. Or choose one tableau for the whole class, with one half 'freezing' and the other adding sound effects.

OBJECTIVES
To enable children to:
■ present drama to others
■ create and sustain roles
■ use language and sound effectively
■ use tableaux to convey situations
■ evaluate performances.

CROSS-CURRICULAR LINKS
PSHE
Developing interpersonal skills; working co-operatively; taking part in discussions; gaining self-confidence; developing cognitive skills.

ENGLISH
Listening to others; taking turns in speaking; discussing and exploring ideas.

Name   Date

Instruction cards

Instruct your partner to:
make a cup of tea without using the words:

water
cup
tea (or *tea-bag*)
kettle
milk

Instruct your partner to:
plant a flower without using the words:

soil
garden
flower
dig
plant

Instruct your partner to:
tie their shoelace without using the words:

shoe
lace
tie
knot
bow

Instruct your partner to:
write a letter without using the words:

paper
pen
letter
envelope
write

Instruct your partner to:
make beans on toast without using the words:

bread
toaster
beans
tin
knife

Instruct your partner to:
clean their teeth without using the words:

teeth
toothbrush
toothpaste
tube
rinse

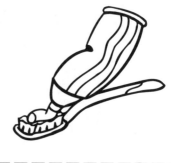

Photocopiables

'Just a minute' subject cards (1)

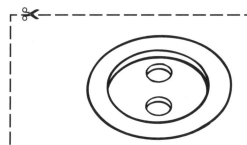

button

banana

elephant

dog

tomato

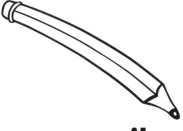

pencil

feather

hat

'Just a minute' subject cards (2)

teddy bear

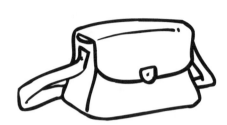

handbag

roller-skates

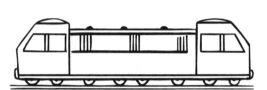

train

ship

telephone

comb

paintbrush

'Just a minute' subject cards (3)

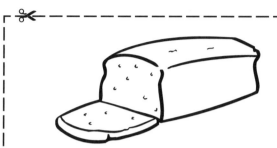

loaf of bread

horse

hairbrush

watch

pig

diamond ring

pair of scissors

sausage

Photocopiables

Freeze titles

Going home

Celebration

Welcome

Lost

Winner takes it all!

The race

Who cares?

Time passes

Ready to go! IDEAS FOR DRAMA

Section 4 DEVELOPING CREATIVE EXPRESSION

The activities in this section focus on children:
■ understanding the concept of mime
■ responding appropriately to the 'freeze' command
■ concentrating on performance elements
■ expressing themselves physically in a creative way
■ responding to creative stimuli
■ learning how to convey characters, situations and emotions through mime and tableaux.

This section begins to focus specifically on the skills required for improvisation and performance. The activities at the beginning encourage children to respond creatively to various stimuli, mostly through mime, then the section goes on to develop their abilities using controlled responses in freezes, or tableaux. This provides a sound basis for the activities in the final section of this book.

MOOD FREEZES

RESOURCES AND LESSON ORGANIZATION

You will need: a large work space; cards from photocopiable page 46; photocopiable pages 10 and 47 (for 'Now or later' activities). Children work individually, then in small groups, then take part in a whole-class discussion.

WHAT TO DO

Ask the children to spread out and find a space to stand in. Explain that they are going to move carefully around the room and, after a while, you are going to call out a mood, feeling or emotion. They should then freeze instantly in the position of someone expressing that mood, feeling or emotion. Tell the children that they can express the mood in a realistic way, as a character in a situation, or in an abstract way by using their bodies to convey the mood.

When all of the children understand what is expected of them, ask them to move carefully around the room, freezing when you give the command. Then ask them to express several different moods, for example happiness, sadness, nervousness, excitement, loneliness, fear, anger, boredom (or alternatives that you choose). Take time to view each freeze, commenting positively where appropriate.

Now ask the children to form groups of up to four, and give each group one of the mood cards, instructing them not to reveal what is written on their card to any of the other groups. Tell them that you want each group to present a freeze, or tableau, that expresses the mood written on their card. Explain that they can represent their mood in any way they like: as a realistic picture or scene, or using abstract positions that convey the emotion. Allow the groups up to three minutes to plan and prepare their freezes.

View each freeze in turn, inviting the rest of the groups, as the audience, to guess the mood shown and to comment on how realistic, expressive and powerful each freeze is.

When all the groups have performed, encourage the children to reflect on the activity by asking them: *Did you enjoy that? Why? Why not? Did you feel that your freezes were expressive? Why? Why not? What do you think you could do to improve your work? Was it acting?* (Yes, because we were using our bodies and faces to convey emotions and situations.)

OBJECTIVES

To enable children to:
■ use body language to convey emotions
■ work in role
■ create and sustain characters
■ present drama to others
■ reflect on and evaluate drama.

CROSS-CURRICULAR LINKS
PSHE

Working co-operatively; gaining self-confidence; developing interpersonal skills; facing challenges; exploring feelings and emotions.

ENGLISH

Listening to others; speaking confidently and clearly; responding appropriately to others; planning and sharing ideas.

NOW OR LATER
■ Challenge the children to represent the moods from cards on photocopiable page 47. These may be more difficult, both to perform and for the audience to work out or guess.
■ Invite the children to suggest other moods. Write these on cards (you could use photocopiable page 10), distribute them and ask the children to create group freezes.
■ Ask the children to create small-group improvisations based on a mood or emotion.
■ Encourage the children to use moods or emotions to create characters and to improvise these in various situations, in pairs or small groups.

IN THE MANNER OF THE WORD

OBJECTIVES
To enable children to:
■ develop basic mime skills
■ use actions effectively and expressively
■ use language as a dramatic stimulus
■ gain self-confidence
■ develop creative responses.

CROSS-CURRICULAR LINKS
PSHE
Following instructions; developing interpersonal skills; taking part in discussions; facing challenges in a supportive environment.

ENGLISH
Developing speaking and listening skills; responding appropriately to others; increasing vocabulary; sharing ideas and experiences.

RESOURCES AND LESSON ORGANIZATION
You will need a medium to large space in which to work. Children work together as a whole class.

WHAT TO DO
Ask the children to sit in a semicircle, facing the classroom door or an area where one child can go out of earshot.

Explain to the children that one of them is going to leave the room (or go where they cannot hear the rest of the class) and that, upon re-entering, they will give the others a simple mime to perform. Remind the children that miming is performing without sounds or words. Whilst the child is absent, ask the rest of the class to select an adverb (a word which describes how something is done) in the manner of which their given mime will be performed. Examples could include: slowly, noisily, angrily, quietly, quickly and so on. The selected adverb must not be revealed to the absent child, who must guess what the adverb chosen is by the manner in which the mime is being performed.

Select your volunteer to leave the room and ask them to think of a suitable simple mime that they will give the other children to perform, for example brushing their teeth, making beans on toast or combing their hair.

Whilst this child is absent, ask the remaining children to choose an appropriate adverb for the mime to be given to them. Make sure they do not discuss this too loudly, in case the other child hears them. When the adverb has been agreed, call the absent child back and ask them to state the mime to be performed. The other children then perform this mime in the manner of the word (adverb) and continue performing until the child correctly guesses the adverb. Allow the guesser three or four attempts, encouraging and guiding them as they get closer to guessing correctly. Once all of the guesses have been used up, or the adverb has been worked out,

praise all of the children and repeat the activity with a different guesser and a new adverb and mime.

After several repetitions, thank and praise the children for their efforts and lead a brief discussion, asking them what skills or new knowledge they have gained from the activity and how these could be applied to other areas of their school life.

NOW OR LATER

- Prepare a list of adverbs for the children to select from.
- Prepare simple mimes on cards for the absent child to select from.
- Use the activity to link to other work on adverbs.
- Select adverbs from a play, story or poem that the children have recently read.
- Ask the children to include all of the different adverbs in a piece of creative writing.

OBJECT MIMES

RESOURCES AND LESSON ORGANIZATION

You will need: a small to medium work space; a comb, pen, torch or similar small object. Children work together as a whole class.

WHAT TO DO

Sit in a circle with the children. Explain that you are going to pass around a familiar object and that each person in turn should mime using this object in a different way. For example, a comb could be used as a telephone, a conductor's baton, a ruler or even a comb! Take a short while to explore the various mimes that the object could be used for. Each child should present a different mime to the rest of the group, responding as quickly as possible when the object reaches them.

Encourage everyone to attempt a mime, advising them to make their movements as clear, realistic and appropriate as possible. When the activity has been completed with one object having been passed around the circle, repeat it with a different one.

Finally, prompt the children to reflect on the activity by asking: *Did you enjoy that? Why? Why not? What did you find difficult about doing it? What skills does this activity teach you?* (To respond spontaneously; to be imaginative; to perform mimes; to use actions and our faces expressively.)

NOW OR LATER

- For less confident children, the option to say, *Pass* could be included.
- Children could be asked to accompany their mimes with sound effects.
- Turn the activity into a game similar to 'pass the parcel', for example by passing the object around the circle to music and asking the person holding the object when the music stops to use it in a different way.

OBJECTIVES

To enable children to:
- develop basic mime skills
- present drama to others
- develop spontaneous creative responses
- use actions to convey ideas
- respond to drama in which they have participated.

CROSS-CURRICULAR LINKS

PSHE

Generating a supportive environment; developing interpersonal skills; facing challenges; taking turns.

ENGLISH

Listening with understanding; sharing ideas and experiences; responding appropriately to others.

MIME THROUGH A WINDOW

OBJECTIVES

To enable children to:
■ use actions to convey roles and situations
■ gain self-confidence
■ respond to drama.

CROSS-CURRICULAR LINKS

PSHE

Working co-operatively; following instructions; developing interpersonal skills; meeting challenges.

ENGLISH

Listening with understanding; sharing and expressing ideas; evaluating drama ideas.

RESOURCES AND LESSON ORGANIZATION

You will need: a medium to large work space; situation cards from photocopiable pages 48 and 49. Children work with partners in a whole-class setting.

WHAT TO DO

Ask two children to stand at the front of the class and tell them to imagine that a big glass window separates them. Explain that one person needs to convey a message to the other, but that this can only be done in mime because speech will not be heard through the window. Tell the children that their messages need to be conveyed clearly and effectively in order for the person on the other side of the window to understand them.

When the two volunteers understand what they need to do, ask one of them to select a card (the text on which should be hidden from their partner) and to mime the message on the card to their partner. Tell the child miming to make their movements large and clear, and to think of as many ways as possible to convey their message. Allow the mime to continue for a few moments and then ask the child watching to guess what the message being conveyed might be. Encourage those children observing as the audience to remain silent at this stage, but if the guesser cannot work out the message correctly, invite the class to suggest what it might be.

If no one guesses the answer on the card, reveal it to the children and then invite suggestions for how this message could have been mimed effectively, allowing one or two children to show their ideas to the rest of the group.

Repeat the process several times, selecting two new children and a different card each time and using each turn to build on the children's physical communication skills.

Finally, encourage the children to think further about their work by asking: *Did you enjoy that? Why? Why not? Was it difficult to do? Why? How could the mimes have been made more understandable?* (By not trying to mime direct translations of what was written on the card, but using symbolic actions to convey the ideas.) *What have you learned from this activity?* (How to convey ideas using movement; to make actions clear and expressive; to use our faces and bodies effectively; to use our imaginations.)

NOW OR LATER

■ Invite the children to suggest other mimes for repetitions of the activity.
■ Develop the concept into a small-group mime, where several people are trying to convey a message to one other person. Then develop these further, where one character deliberately misunderstands what is being communicated to them.

FREEZE OBJECTS

RESOURCES AND LESSON ORGANIZATION
You will need: a large work space; a whistle. Children work in small groups.

WHAT TO DO
Ask the children to spread out and walk carefully around the room, moving continuously into empty floor space and not touching or bumping into anyone else. After a short while, blow the whistle and call out a number between one and ten. (It is advisable to begin with a number that your class can be divided into equally if possible). Ask the children to form groups of that number as quickly as possible.

Repeat the process, asking the children to walk around the room and calling out another number. This time give the children a countdown from ten for them to form their groups. Now tell the children that you are going to ask them to walk around the room again before calling out a (small) group size and stating an object for them to make with their bodies in their groups.

When the children are in their groups, ask them to make the shape of a car, using their bodies only and working together as a group. Allow the children a few seconds to discuss and begin planning and then give them a countdown from ten. After the count of 'one' tell the children to freeze in their group positions, instructing them to be completely still and silent, and walk around the room viewing each of the car freezes, giving praise where appropriate.

Repeat the process with other group sizes and objects, for example a bed, piano, telephone, television, aeroplane (or alternatives of your choice) to develop their responses to the 'freeze' command and encourage stillness and silence.

Finally, encourage the children to reflect on the activity by asking them: *Did you enjoy that? Why? Why not? Which object did you find the most difficult to make? Why? What do you think the session taught you?* (To work together; to respond quickly; to use our imaginations; to use our bodies expressively; to respond to the 'freeze' command.)

NOW OR LATER
■ Reduce the time limit by counting down only from five.
■ Using the same process, ask the children to form geometric shapes, such as a square, a circle, and a triangle.
■ Ask the children to form letters of the alphabet in their groups.
■ See if the groups can form the shapes of different animals.
■ Invite suggestions from the children for other shapes or objects that they could form in their groups.

OBJECTIVES
To enable children to:
■ respond spontaneously to instructions
■ use their bodies effectively
■ develop freeze skills
■ work co-operatively
■ develop creative expression.

CROSS-CURRICULAR LINKS
PSHE
Developing interpersonal skills; taking part in discussions; contributing to group work; facing challenges.

ENGLISH
Listening to other people; responding appropriately to others; sharing ideas and experiences; evaluating ideas in drama.

ART GALLERY

OBJECTIVES

To enable children to:
■ develop creative expression
■ gain self-confidence
■ present drama to others
■ use actions expressively
■ work well with others.

CROSS-CURRICULAR LINKS

PSHE

Developing interpersonal skills; generating a supportive atmosphere; developing cognitive skills; following instructions.

ENGLISH

Listening to others; sharing ideas and experiences; planning and evaluating; responding appropriately to others.

ART

Appreciating the different ways in which ideas, feelings and meanings are communicated in visual form.

RESOURCES AND LESSON ORGANIZATION

You will need a large space in which to work. Children work in pairs and then participate in a whole-class discussion.

WHAT TO DO

Ask the children to find a partner and stand in a space. (If you have an odd number of children in the group, one pair can work as a three.) Explain that they are going to create an art gallery full of sculptures. Lead a brief discussion, asking: *What is a sculpture?* (A three-dimensional work of art.) *What are sculptures made of?* (Clay, wood, marble, bronze and so on.) *What sort of things do sculptures represent?* (Human beings, objects, scenes and situations, emotions, abstract ideas…)

Explain to the children that they are going to work with their partners to form their bodies into a sculpted work of art. Tell them to decide what material their sculpture is made of, what it represents, whether it is realistic or abstract and ask the children to, finally, give their sculpture a name or title.

Allow the children up to three minutes to discuss, plan and prepare their sculpture-freezes, giving them regular updates on the time remaining. When the time limit has expired ask the children to position their sculptures in a space and instruct them to freeze in position. Walk around the room, asking each pair what the name or title of their sculpture is. Encourage children waiting to be seen to remain still and silent, as if they really were pieces of work in an art gallery.

When you have looked at all the sculptures, ask the children to relax and reflect together on the activity. Ask them: *Did you enjoy that? Why? Why not? How did you feel about your sculpture? Were you happy with the final result? What would you change about it if you had the chance? What was the most difficult part of the activity?* (This is usually deciding on the name of their sculpture.) *What do you think you have learned from doing that activity?* (How to work together; to use our imaginations; to be creative with our bodies; to remain still and silent for a long time.)

NOW OR LATER

■ Use the final evaluation to allow children to recreate and refine their sculptures.
■ Invite each half of the class to view the sculptures created by the others.
■ Give the art exhibition an overall theme or title, so that all the pairs create sculptures that interpret a common idea.
■ Help the children to recreate pictures of actual sculptures from art books, photographs or postcards.

SITUATION FREEZES

RESOURCES AND LESSON ORGANIZATION

You will need a large space in which to work. Children work together as a whole class.

WHAT TO DO

Tell the children that they are going to create a whole-class frozen picture of a scene or situation of their choosing. Explain that one child will be asked to leave the room (or go where they cannot see or hear what is happening) and will then be brought back in to guess what the scene or situation is that has been created in the freeze.

Ask one child to leave and ask the remaining group members what scene or situation they would like to create a freeze of. Examples could include a hospital, railway station, birthday party, wedding and funeral. The scene selected needs to involve the whole group in various roles as characters within the picture.

When the children have decided what situation they want to create, encourage them to find positions in the room where they can represent people involved in the picture, making sure that only one space is assigned for each area of the scene, and that children do not duplicate sections of the picture. For example, if the children are creating a hospital, allocate one area of the room as the waiting room, another area as the operating theatre, a third as a ward, and so on.

Allow the children up to two minutes to create their situation and then give the 'freeze' command, instructing them to be completely still and silent. Ask the absent child to return and to guess what situation the freeze represents. When they have guessed correctly repeat the process with another volunteer and a different scene.

Finally, encourage the children to reflect on the activity by asking: *Did you enjoy that? Why? Why not? What was the most difficult part of the activity?* (Often this is deciding what situation to create!) *What do you think you learned?* (To work together; to be creative; to use our faces and bodies expressively; to think about space and positioning when creating freezes.)

NOW OR LATER

■ Invite suggestions for ideas of other situations to be performed, write these on slips of paper and draw them out at random.
■ Ask the children to create whole-class freezes of scenes from familiar stories, inviting the absent child to guess which story they represent.

OBJECTIVES

To enable children to:
■ use actions to convey situations and roles
■ develop skills in creating tableaux
■ work in role
■ present drama to others.

CROSS-CURRICULAR LINKS
PSHE

Working co-operatively; facing challenges in a positive and supportive environment; gaining self-confidence; contributing to group work.

ENGLISH

Listening to others; discussing possibilities; responding appropriately to others; evaluating ideas in drama.

Mood cards (1)

anger

hope

fear

excitement

sadness

happiness

loneliness

contentment

Mood cards (2)

boredom   **panic**

joy   **confusion**

envy   **nervousness**

triumph   **love**

Photocopiables

'Mime through a window' cards (1)

Your roof is on fire.	Your dog has been in my garden and dug up my flower bed.
I've got a big, heavy parcel to deliver to you.	Do you want any milk?
I've come to read your gas meter.	There's been a car accident and I need to ring the emergency services.
I've locked myself out of my house. Can you help me?	I'm collecting for the local charity shop. Do you have any items to give away?

'Mime through a window' cards (2)

There's a gas leak and the street is being evacuated.	Your car is blocking my drive. Could you move it, please?
I'm canvassing on behalf of a political party. Can we count on your vote?	I'm from the Scouts/Guides. Do you want any jobs done?
Your guinea pig has escaped.	Do you want your windows cleaned?
I need you to sign for this important letter.	Your cat is stuck up a tree.

 **ROLE-PLAY, IMPROVISATION AND PERFORMANCE SKILLS**

The activities in this section focus on children:
■ understanding the basics of scripts and character work
■ creating and sustaining roles
■ exploring well-known and unfamiliar characters
■ experiencing creative performance
■ presenting drama to others
■ creating stories.
   These activities bring together the work covered in the previous sections. They focus primarily on the aspects of drama associated with working in role, improvisation, performance and presentation, allowing the children more opportunity for constructive assessment of their own work and that of others.

SIMPLE SCRIPTS

OBJECTIVES

To enable children to:
■ work in role
■ develop scenes or incidents
■ develop improvisation skills
■ use character, action and dialogue to convey ideas in scripted performances
■ present and evaluate drama.

CROSS-CURRICULAR LINKS

PSHE

Gaining self-confidence; developing interpersonal skills; developing cognitive skills; speaking confidently in front of an audience.

ENGLISH

Listening to others; speaking confidently and clearly; responding appropriately to others; evaluating ideas in responding to drama; reading aloud.

RESOURCES AND LESSON ORGANIZATION

You will need: a medium to large work space; a copy of the script on photocopiable pages 58–9 for each child. Children work in pairs, then in small groups, and then as a whole class.

WHAT TO DO

Ask the children to find a partner and a space to work in. Read through the script whilst the children follow on their copies. Ask the children to work with their partners to read, discuss and rehearse a performance of the script. Encourage them to consider such aspects as:
■ vocal expression and intonation
■ using body language to reflect what they are saying
■ using body language to counter what they are saying
■ using appropriate facial expressions
■ positioning (for example, facing the audience, relating to other characters, defining the space)
■ creating mood and tension.

   Explain to the children that you will allow them up to five minutes to discuss, plan and rehearse their performances of the script and then each one will be presented to the rest of the class. Give regular updates on the time remaining and move between the pairs, providing advice and guidance where required. When the time limit has elapsed, designate an area of the room as the performance area and watch each pair perform their version of the simple script.

   Use these performances as an evaluation process, asking the children such questions as: *Was that realistic? Why? Why not? How believable were the characters? What did you think about the use of vocal expression? Did that performance make you want to know what happened next?*

   Now ask the children to form groups of three or four and tell them that you want them to improvise what happened next, explaining that two additional characters should enter the scene and that the situation can be developed in any way that the children wish. Lead a brief discussion, asking: *Who could the two additional characters be?* (One would be Sally; others could include Mrs Thompson, Mr Clarke, Joseph, Chloe or alternatives of the children's choosing.)

   Allow the children up to ten minutes to discuss, plan, prepare and rehearse their improvised additional scenes and then view each performance in turn, again assessing the content, skill of performance and realism of each one.

Finally, encourage the children all together to reflect on the session. Ask them: *Did you enjoy that activity? Why? Why not? Did you find it difficult to act as the characters? How did you decide what happened next? Can you think of any other endings for the scene? How can we tell what sort of people these characters are?* (By what they say, how they say things and how they react towards other characters.)

NOW OR LATER
■ Use other endings suggested by the children as a basis for further improvisation.
■ Use the evaluation as an opportunity for children to assess and refine their performances.
■ Ask the children to improvise other scenes: before the script picks up the story; Sally's home; Chloe and other children; the school playground, and so on.
■ Invite the children to name the two friends, write up their improvisations in scripted form and give titles to their short plays.

HOT-SEATING

RESOURCES AND LESSON ORGANIZATION
You will need: a small to medium work space; a copy of the script on photocopiable pages 58–9 for each child; a chair to be the 'hot seat'; small items of clothing as 'costume' (optional). Children work as a whole class.

WHAT TO DO
Sit at the front of the room, or with the children in a circle. Re-read the script with the children. Encourage them to focus on the characters from the scene by prompting with questions about what sort of person Friend 1 is and if they have any other friends. What about Sally? Ask: *How old do you think these children are? Was Sally right to hit Joseph? Why do you think Chloe says nasty things about other people? Do you think the teachers know what is happening? Do you think Sally heard what was being said about her? How do you think she reacted when she entered?*

Now explain to the children that they are going to have the opportunity to ask one of the characters from the scene some questions, saying: *If you could talk to one of the characters, who would it be and what would you want to know?* When you have acknowledged several responses, select one of the suggested characters as a role to adopt, bring forward a chair and tell the children that you are now going to be that character and will answer their questions. (Although going into role is more about

Ready to go! IDEAS FOR DRAMA

adopting an attitude than becoming another person, a clear distinction needs to be made between you as yourself and as the character. This could involve simply sitting on the chair in a manner specific to the character, or donning an appropriate item of clothing as a token costume.)

Invite the children to ask any questions they want to put to your character, encouraging them to raise their hands, take turns in asking and speak clearly. If children find it difficult to control their questioning, or become noisy, come out of role by either standing up or removing your costume and say something like: *I would like to know more about… (the character), but we won't find out anything unless we ask questions properly and listen carefully to the answers.* Adopt your role again and respond as the character to each question asked, remaining in character regardless of the questions posed, and repeating answers if necessary. Continue until all questions have been asked and then come out of role again.

Encourage the children to reflect on the activity by asking: *What did you learn about that character that you didn't know before? Were there any other questions that you could have asked? Will knowing the answers make it easier for you to act as that character?* (Yes, because when we know and understand characters, we can act as them more realistically.)

NOW OR LATER

■ Repeat the process with other characters from the script.
■ Ask the children to prepare their questions in groups before beginning the hot-seating session.
■ Invite some of the children to answer questions in role as characters from the script.
■ Ask the children to record their questions, and the answers, in writing.
■ Working in pairs, ask the children to interview each other: one child taking on the role of a child from the script, the other the role of the headteacher. These interviews can then be written up as reports for the school.

TELEVISION NEWS

OBJECTIVES

To enable children to:
■ present drama to an audience
■ improvise and work in role
■ develop creative presentation skills
■ follow and respond to instructions
■ perform improvisations.

CROSS-CURRICULAR LINKS
PSHE

Working co-operatively; taking part in discussions; developing cognitive skills; developing interpersonal skills; contributing to group work.

ENGLISH

Listening and responding to other people; discussing and planning ideas; increasing vocabulary; speaking confidently and clearly; sharing experiences; creating news reports.

RESOURCES AND LESSON ORGANIZATION

You will need: a medium to large work space; a copy of photocopiable page 57 for each group; writing materials; paper; desk or table; chairs; other 'television news' props as required (for example weather chart, microphones, cameras); a 'newsflash' sheet with an important story (see 'What to do'). Children work in small groups then participate in a whole-class discussion.

WHAT TO DO

Organize the children into groups of up to six and explain that they are going to create a television news programme. Read through the headlines with the children. Ask them: *Which story do you think is the most important? Which news story would be told in the greatest detail? What sort of information could you write and present on each of these stories? How many presenters could you have? What else could be included in your programme?* (Sport and weather bulletins.)

Tell the children that you would like them to devise, write and present a television news programme lasting five minutes and including as many of the news stories from the headlines as possible. Explain that their programmes must have a title, at least one presenter and at least two interviews with people involved in the stories, with one interview being conducted away from the studio (as an outside broadcast). Inform the children that you will allow up to 15 minutes for them to discuss, plan, prepare and rehearse their television programmes and that then you will view each presentation in turn.

Whilst the children are preparing their news programmes, set up an area of the room as the television studio – complete with desk, or table, chairs and any other studio props you choose to use. Give the children regular updates on the amount of time remaining and move regularly from group to group, providing support and resolving any disagreements.

When only three minutes remain, present each group with the 'newsflash' sheet: a recently reported important item, such as 'The Queen has announced her decision to abdicate, but Prince William, not Prince Charles, is to take over the throne.' Explain that their programmes must include this important news. Encourage the children to decide how this new headline will be included in their programmes, how much precedence it will take over other stories, what stories will be dropped in favour of it and how the

format of their programme will now change. Remind the children that they only have three minutes remaining until they are 'on air', and encourage them to resolve this problem quickly and efficiently.

When the time limit has elapsed, firmly instruct the children to stop rehearsing and ask each group in turn to present their television news programme, positioning themselves in the 'studio'. Invite the children observing as an audience to make constructive comments after each presentation by asking such questions as: *Was that realistic? Do you feel they covered the important stories? How well do you think the programme was presented? How could they have made it better? What do you feel they did well? Which aspect of the programme was particularly effective or well presented?*

Now or later
■ Use the evaluations as a basis for the children to refine their presentations.
■ Ask the children to create television news stories based upon other headlines: school events; world events; events from history.

Last-line improvisations

Resources and lesson organization
You will need: a large work space; cards from photocopiable page 60. Children work together in small groups.

What to do
Ask the children to form groups of up to six and tell them that each group is going to devise a short improvisation, or play, which they will perform to the rest of the class. Explain that each of these improvisations will have to *end* with a specific line, given on a card and that their scenes must lead up to the closing line they select.

Turn the cards face down and ask each group to select one. Do not allow groups to change their cards once their 'last lines' have been selected! Inform the children that they have a maximum of ten minutes to discuss, plan, prepare and rehearse their performances and encourage them to think about sequencing events realistically, developing and sustaining their roles and creating believable endings. Advise the children that their performances must not last longer than three minutes.

When all of the children understand what is expected of them and have begun their preparations, move quickly from group to group, giving support and resolving any difficulties. Give the children regular updates on the time remaining and, when the time limit has elapsed, designate an area of the room as the performance area

Objectives
To enable children to:
■ create, sequence and develop scenes and events
■ work in role
■ present drama to others
■ create and sustain roles
■ evaluate performances.

CROSS-CURRICULAR LINKS
PSHE
Developing interpersonal skills; facing challenges; contributing to group work; gaining self-confidence.

ENGLISH
Listening to others; speaking confidently and clearly; responding appropriately to others; sharing ideas and experiences; evaluating ideas in responding to drama.

and view each improvisation in turn.

Invite the children observing as an audience to make constructive comments after each presentation. Ask questions such as: *Was that performance realistic? Did you believe in the character and events? How well do you think it was presented? How could they have made it more interesting, realistic or effective? What do you feel was good about the play? Which characters did you find interesting or well portrayed?* Children who have just performed could also be asked for their assessment: *How did you think that went? Were you happy with what you achieved? Why? Why not? What would you change if you had the opportunity? What did you find the most difficult part of devising your performance?*

NOW OR LATER
■ Use the evaluations as a basis for children to refine and re-present their improvisations.
■ Invite the children to suggest alternative last lines and create new improvisations from them.
■ Ask the children to create additional scenes for their plays – either before or after the scene performed.
■ Ask the children to write up their plays in scripted form.
■ Use the same process for creating 'first-line improvisations', with groups devising short plays that have to begin with a specified first line.

MATILDA

OBJECTIVES
To enable children to:
■ respond in role to create stories
■ present drama to others
■ use actions to convey situations, characters and emotions
■ create and sustain roles
■ respond to performances.

RESOURCES AND LESSON ORGANIZATION
You will need: a large work space; the poem on photocopiable page 61. Children work as individuals, in pairs, and in small groups, then as a whole class.

WHAT TO DO
Read through the poem, 'Matilda'. Explore the poem by asking the children how old they think Matilda is. What sort of person is she? What sort of person is her Aunt? How does she feel about Matilda? Then encourage the children to consider how the poem could be presented visually by asking: *How could we perform the poem using movement and narration only?* (People playing the characters could act out the story as it is read.) *What parts of the poem would work well in mime?* (All of it could be

mimed.) *How could we show the different characters and their roles through movement only?* (Matilda could be mimed being sneaky and sly; her Aunt could be mimed being fed up and cross with her; the fire brigade could be mimed rushing around Matilda's house and climbing ladders, and the crowd and people in the street could react to what Matilda was doing.)

Explain that, as you read the poem out loud, the children should respond with appropriate mimed actions to accompany the narrative. Select two children to act out the roles of Matilda and her Aunt, eight to perform as the fire brigade, up to fourteen to play the 'frenzied crowd', and the remaining children to act as the 'people passing in the street'. Ensure that all of the children understand their roles and what is expected of them.

Encourage the children playing townspeople to devise characters for themselves, either individually or in pairs. Advise the children to listen carefully to your narration and to react with appropriate movements at the correct moment. When all of the children are ready, begin reading the poem and continue slowly, allowing time for the children to react as their characters.

When completed, this performance can be refined by directing the children to provide specific moves, or by including some dialogue, such as: the fire brigade calling out in unison, *Matilda's house is burning down!*; Matilda calling out, *Fire!*; and the people passing in the street answering together, *Little Liar!*

Finally, encourage the children to reflect on their work by asking: *How do you feel about your performance? What do you think you could have done better? What do you feel went well? What would you change about the performance if you had the chance to repeat it? Why?* This final response could be used for further development of the performance of 'Matilda' and encourages the children to appreciate their personal performance skills and the concept of presenting work to an audience.

NOW OR LATER

■ Ask the children to enact the poem using a narrator and a series of freezes only, each freeze showing a different scene.
■ Encourage the children to improvise conversations between characters: Matilda and her Aunt; Matilda's Aunt and members of the fire brigade; members of the fire brigade; members of the public, and so on.
■ The children could enact the poem using a combination of freezes, mime and improvised dialogue.

CROSS-CURRICULAR LINKS
PSHE
Working co-operatively; listening to others; following rules; taking part in discussions.

ENGLISH
Speaking to different people; sharing ideas and experiences; acting out poems; responding imaginatively to what they read; exploring rhyme.

Section 5

CHARACTER ADVERTS

OBJECTIVES

To enable children to:
■ develop improvisation skills
■ create and sustain roles
■ present drama to others
■ use character, action and narrative to convey ideas
■ respond to performances.

CROSS-CURRICULAR LINKS

PSHE

Developing interpersonal skills; taking part in discussions; gaining self-confidence; speaking confidently in front of an audience.

ENGLISH

Listening to others; speaking clearly and confidently; sharing ideas and experiences; using language effectively; responding appropriately to others.

RESOURCES AND LESSON ORGANIZATION

You will need: a medium to large work space; cards from photocopiable pages 62–3. Children work together in pairs or small groups.

WHAT TO DO

Ask the children to form pairs or groups of up to four. Explain that they are going to create short television advertisements to perform to the rest of the group. Tell them that these advertisements will be based on characters written on the cards. Explain that each group will select a character card and will devise their television advertisement based on something connected with that particular character. For example, a group selecting the card 'cowboy' might devise and present an advertisement for a lasso, a cowboy hat, horse-riding lessons, jeans and so on.

Advise the children that their improvised television advertisements must not last any longer than one minute, that every member of their group must be involved and that the product being promoted must be directly linked to the character on the card they have selected.

When all of the children understand what is expected of them, turn the character cards face down and ask each pair or group to select a card. Do not allow any cards to be exchanged once they have been chosen!

Inform the children that they have ten minutes to discuss, plan, prepare and rehearse their character adverts, and, as they are working, give them regular updates on the time remaining. When the time limit has elapsed, ask each group to show their character advert in turn, encouraging audience members to remain silent whilst watching and leading a round of applause for each performance.

When all of the advertisements have been seen, encourage the children to reflect on the activity by asking them questions, such as: *Did you enjoy doing that? Why? Why not? Which was the most persuasive advert? Which was the most realistic advert? If you could change anything about your performance, what would that be? What do you think you have learned from doing this activity?* (To perform in front of others; to use language effectively; to create characters and roles; to use our imaginations; to give our improvisations a purpose.)

NOW OR LATER

■ Use the evaluation as an opportunity for children to refine their improvisations.
■ Invite the children to suggest other characters to use as a basis for creating television advertisements.
■ Ask the children to create advertisements for everyday products, such as washing-up liquid, chocolate and shampoo.
■ Help the children to create a complete advertising campaign for a new product, from posters to television presentations.

News headlines

1. Girls are achieving better exam results than boys.

2. A painting by Van Gogh has sold at auction for £24 million.

3. Nurses are considering strike action over poor pay deals.

4. British athletes have won a record number of medals at the Olympic Games.

5. The government's loan system for university students is to be abolished.

6. A British film director has been nominated for an Oscar.

7. A woman missed out on a major lottery win – because her husband forgot to buy the ticket!

Simple script

FRIEND 1:   Have you heard about Sally?

FRIEND 2:   No. What?

FRIEND 1:   Well, I heard Mrs Thompson telling Mr Clarke that she's got to go and see the head.

FRIEND 2:   What for? What's she done?

FRIEND 1:   She's been fighting.

FRIEND 2:   Fighting? Who's she been fighting? What sort of fighting?

FRIEND 1:   Mrs Thompson caught her smacking Joseph in the face.

FRIEND 2:   No!

FRIEND 1:   Yeah! I heard her talking about it.

FRIEND 2:   Why did she smack Joseph?

FRIEND 1:   Dunno.

FRIEND 2:   You're making it up.

FRIEND 1:   I'm not. It's true! I saw Joseph crying all over the place afterwards.

FRIEND 2:   Did you?

FRIEND 1:   Well, sort of. Chloe told me about it, anyway.

FRIEND 2:   Oh, Chloe. She tells stories about everyone. Anyway, Joseph deserves to get smacked; he's always saying nasty things to people.

FRIEND 1:   I know. *(Pause)* I wonder what he said to Sally.

FRIEND 2:   I bet it was something about her dad.

FRIEND 1:   Yeah. That's mean, that is.

FRIEND 2:   Joseph must have said something really horrible to make Sally hit him.

FRIEND 1:   Yeah. I think it's rotten to say horrible things like that.

FRIEND 2:   Me too.

FRIEND 1:   I wouldn't ever say horrible things like that to people.

FRIEND 2:   Me neither. It's not right.

FRIEND 1:   Anyway, Sally's going to be in big trouble now.

FRIEND 2:   Well, whatever he said, she shouldn't have hit him.

FRIEND 1:   No, she shouldn't. My mum always says if anyone is nasty to you, just walk away.

FRIEND 2:   Yeah. My mum says that too. That's what I'd have done.

FRIEND 1:   Me too. Sally should have just walked away.

FRIEND 2:   Yeah. *(Pause)* I'm going to find Chloe. You coming?

They both turn to go and come face to face with Sally.
Pause.

FRIEND 1:   Oh! *(Pause)* Hello, Sally.

Last lines

What on earth was that?!

I never want to see another Liquorice Allsort again!

Thanks, but can I have my pyjamas back, please?

Well, at least my toothache's gone.

I told you not to call him Gladys!

So, you must be the rightful king of England.

That's not raspberry juice, you idiot, that's blood.

Farewell. I must return to my own time.

Matilda

(who told lies and was burned to death)

Matilda told such Dreadful Lies,
It made one Gasp and Stretch one's Eyes;
Her Aunt, who from her Earliest Youth,
Had kept a Strict Regard for Truth,
Attempted to Believe Matilda:
The effort very nearly killed her,
And would have done so, had not She
Discovered this Infirmity.
For once, towards the Close of Day,
Matilda, growing tired of play,
And finding she was left alone,
Went tiptoe to the Telephone
And summoned the Immediate Aid
Of London's Noble Fire Brigade.
Within an hour the Gallant Band
Were pouring in on every hand,
From Putney, Hackney Downs and Bow,
With Courage high and Hearts aglow,
They galloped, roaring through the Town,
"Matilda's House is Burning Down!"
Inspired by British Cheers and Loud
Proceeding from the Frenzied Crowd,
They ran their ladders through a score
Of windows on the Ball Room Floor;
And took Particular Pains to Souse
The Pictures up and down the House,

Until Matilda's Aunt succeeded
In showing them they were not needed
And even then she had to pay
To get the Men to go away!

****

It happened that a few Weeks later
Her Aunt was off to the Theatre
To see that Interesting Play
The Second Mrs Tanqueray.
She had refused to take her Niece
To hear that Entertaining Piece:
A Deprivation Just and Wise
To Punish her for Telling Lies.
That Night a fire *did* break out –
You should have heard Matilda Shout!
You should have heard her Scream and Bawl,
And throw the window up and call
To People passing in the Street –
(The rapidly increasing Heat
Encouraging her to obtain
Their confidence) – but all in vain!
For every time She shouted "Fire!"
They only answered "Little Liar!"
And therefore when her Aunt returned,
Matilda, and the House, were Burned.

Hillaire Belloc

Character cards (1)

 cowboy

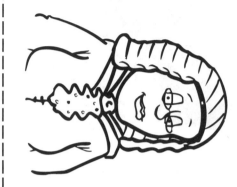 judge

 police officer

 ballerina

 bank robber

 hairdresser

jockey

 postman

Name

Date

Character cards (2)

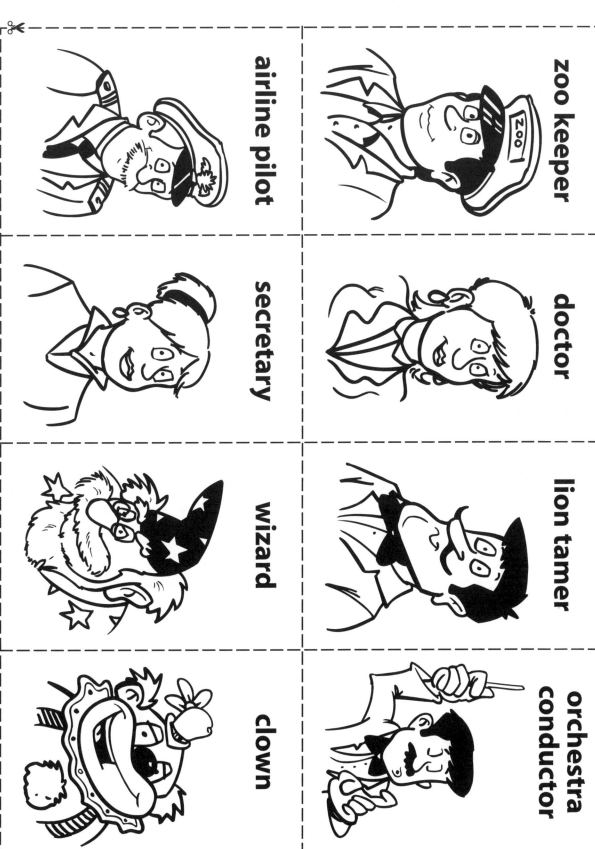

zoo keeper

airline pilot

doctor

secretary

lion tamer

wizard

orchestra conductor

clown

Ready to go! IDEAS FOR DRAMA

NATIONAL STANDARDS FOR KEY SKILLS

The grid below will help you to identify which activities can be used to develop specific key skills, and enable you to check on the overall balance of skill development in your teaching programme. These skills are based on the QCA's National Standards for Key Skills (and the revised orders for the English curriculum).

SKILLS DEVELOPED IN SECTIONS	1	2	3	4	5
Working positively with others	✔	✔	✔	✔	✔
Following specific instructions	✔	✔	✔	✔	✔
Developing communication skills	✔	✔	✔	✔	✔
Using actions to convey situations, characters and emotions		✔	✔	✔	✔
Responding as themselves in a fictional setting		✔	✔	✔	✔
Creating and sustaining roles individually		✔	✔	✔	✔
Creating and sustaining roles when working with others		✔	✔	✔	✔
Using language to convey situations, characters and emotions			✔	✔	✔
Presenting drama to others			✔	✔	✔
Improvising and working in role			✔	✔	✔
Developing scenes, events or incidents				✔	✔
Using conventions to explore characters					✔
Commenting constructively on drama in which they have participated		✔	✔	✔	✔
Commenting constructively on drama they have watched				✔	✔